D1489525

CAREERS IN COMPUTER TECHNOLOGY™

CAREERS IN
Computer Science
AND Programming

JERI FREEDMAN

ROSEN
PUBLISHING

NEW YORK

Published in 2011 by The Rosen Publishing Group, Inc.
29 East 21st Street, New York, NY 10010

First Edition

Library of Congress Cataloging-in-Publication Data

Freedman, Jeri.
Careers in computer science and programming/Jeri Freedman. – 1st ed.
    p. cm. – (Careers in computer technology)
Includes bibliographical references and index.   •
ISBN 978-1-4488-1318-6 (library binding)
1. Computer science–Vocational guidance–Juvenile literature. 2.
Computer programming–Vocational guidance–Juvenile literature. I. Title.
QA76.25.F72 2011
004.023–dc22

                                                        2010012566

Manufactured in the United States of America

CPSIA Compliance Information: Batch #W11YA: For further information, contact Rosen Publishing, New York, New York, at 1-800-237-9932.

On the cover: This software engineer is hard at work at Google's facility in Kirkland, Washington, in 2009.

Contents

Computer technology is an integral part of every aspect of modern life. People rely on computer technology for entertainment, information, and staying in touch with friends, colleagues, and family. Computer games, Web sites, streaming video, downloadable music, texting, and social networking sites such as Facebook and Twitter have become a standard part of many people's lives.

Few industries have affected people's lives as much as the computer industry, and few offer the same prospect of innovation in the future. The fascinating, rapidly changing world of computer technology has fueled many people's interest in a career in this field. This book provides the information necessary to evaluate the different types of computer science and programming careers available. It looks at the variety of different kinds of computer science and programming jobs, and examines the education and training necessary to qualify for them. In addition, it provides practical advice on steps a person can take to obtain each kind of job. People who have studied computer science and programming often find that their skills apply to jobs in a wide variety of fields. Finally, it provides a look at what working in computer science and programming might be like on a day-to-day basis.

Working in computer science and programming can be exciting, and computer professionals are often on the cutting edge of new technological breakthroughs. Working in this field can also be financially rewarding, since such jobs often pay high salaries. At the same time, careers in computer science and programming are often demanding and require long hours of meticulous work and unwavering attention to detail.

There is a steady demand for people with backgrounds in computer science and programming, and this field can provide more job security than many other career paths. A vast number of industries require the skills of computer programmers. In fact, there has never been a time when the demand for those with expertise in computer science and programming has been greater. However, the people who work in this field need to update their skills constantly. Otherwise, they run the risk of falling behind the continual changes in hardware and software technology.

CHAPTER 1

The World of Computing

The field of computer science and programming encompasses the creation, modification, and maintenance of computer software and systems. Professionals in this field may work directly in programming or in related areas of computer technology that rely on a knowledge of computer languages and computer engineering. The roots of computer science and programming date back to World War II (1939–1945). During this time, the first modern computers were created. These initial computers were used primarily by the military and were not available for general use. Computers first became commercially available in the 1950s and were used primarily by large organizations. These computers were enormous and had very little processing power compared to those in use today. They were different from today's desktop computers in the sense that they were mainframes, or very large computers that users interfaced with through terminals, which are monitor and keyboard units with no processing capability of their own.

COMPUTER LANGUAGES

Computers are useless without instructions to tell them to do something. Early programmers encoded instructions for computers by punching holes in cardboard strips called punch cards. Over time, increasingly sophisticated computer languages were

People who enjoy working independently and solving problems are often drawn to computer science and programming careers.

developed, and mainframes graduated from using punch cards to using programs recorded on large spools of magnetic tape.

Computer languages consist of standardized commands that can be combined to create instructions telling a computer how to process data. In the early days of computers, programmers used simple programming languages, such as assembly language, that directly told the computer how to process data at a very basic level. Early programming languages were composed of numbers and symbols that were very hard for people to understand.

Over the succeeding decades, computers became progressively smaller and more powerful. Programming languages such as Pascal, COBOL, and Fortran were developed for business and scientific applications. Floppy disks, zip drives, hard drives, compact discs, and DVDs provided more convenient data storage. Today, the most commonly used computers are desktop personal computers (PCs), and data is generally stored on hard drives or USB drives. Sophisticated computer languages now allow programmers to simply tell a computer what they want it to do. The programming language translates this information into lower-level instructions, simplifying the creation of computer software.

In businesses today, it is common to connect a number of PCs together to allow users to interact with each other and access a central source of data. This arrangement is called a computer network. Computer networks generally connect all the PCs in the network to a central server. A server is a powerful computer that provides more storage capacity and processing power than a typical desktop PC. Computer networks require organization and special security hardware and software that control access to the system.

PROGRAMMING LANGUAGES

A wide variety of special programming languages have been developed for particular applications. Web sites are often built with hyptertext markup language (HTML), extensible markup language (XML), cascading style sheets (CSS), Active Server Pages.NET (ASP.NET), Java, and JavaScript. HTML contains commands that tell a computer how the elements of a Web page should appear on-screen. XML allows programmers to provide increased functionality in Web pages by identifying different types of content in the Web page. CSS provides commands that format Web pages. ASP.NET, Java, and JavaScript allow programmers to add functionality to Web pages so that users can interact with them. Databases, or collections of data organized into digital records and files, frequently use structured query language (SQL) or Oracle software. These languages not only allow the creation of records, but they also allow users to query the database for information. A query is a question or request for information. Computer programmers will encounter many programming languages over the course of their careers.

Complete software programs that perform a specific function are called applications. Examples of commonly used applications are Microsoft Word, Adobe Reader, and Google Maps. The world of programming offers a vast variety of careers, from writing programs to run cars, manufacturing robots, or entire production lines, to creating business and scientific tools that analyze massive amounts of data, or programming video games or the software that creates a special effect in a feature film.

Each type of computer language is generally used for a specific purpose. Languages commonly used in writing computer applications include C+, C++, and Visual Basic. These are object-oriented languages, which place low-level instructions inside of units of code called objects. Today, most programmers use object-oriented programming languages when developing applications. These languages enable programmers to use objects when writing programs to tell computers how to perform tasks, without requiring the programmer to detail every basic activity.

CAREER OUTLOOK

According to the 2010–2011 edition of the U.S. Department of Labor's handbook, jobs in information technology are expected to continue to grow throughout the next decade, despite the downturn in the economy in 2008 and 2009. Companies offering data-processing services and hosting services are projected to experience growth.

Hosting involves providing and running servers for companies that don't want to maintain their own in-house servers. Mobile computing (or the use of wireless technology and small devices such as smartphones and tablet computers that can easily be carried around) is likely to create a demand for a vast number of applications. Mobile devices, such as iPods, netbook computers, and smartphones like the iPhone and BlackBerry, all use applications that are created by programmers. Companies are likely to continue trying to develop new mobile devices for some time to come. The demand for both new applications and those adapted from desktop editions will provide a great deal of work for programmers in the future. The spread of computer networking has created a variety of new programming and computer science careers.

Few industries offer more career opportunities than computer science and programming, and these opportunities are increasing in a number of different industries. One area of expansion is Internet publishing and broadcasting. Online versions of newspapers and magazines are replacing their print cousins. As publishers figure out ways to charge for their products, they are likely to focus more on online versions of their publications.

The health care industry has been experiencing continual growth. Government initiatives to computerize all medical records, as well as increasing interest on the part of hospitals in improving the efficiency of health care delivery, are likely to result in an increased demand for computer science and programming professionals.

Security at all levels is also likely to be a growth industry over the next decade. Designing, programming, and operating electronic security systems will provide ample employment opportunities for people. These might include giant databases that screen for terrorists, biometric identification systems (electronic systems that use physical attributes for identification, such as palm prints or scans of the eye), or intrusion detection systems.

These are just a few of the growing industries that will provide employment for computer professionals—especially those with a background in computer science and programming. Almost every industry is incorporating computer technology into its processes. Chances are, if a person is interested in working in a particular industry, he or she can find computer science or programming jobs in that field.

CHAPTER 2

Careers in Computer Science and Programming

There are many different types of computer science and programming jobs. Having a background in computer science and programming can qualify a person for a wide variety of jobs. Some people choose to seek out a career path that is academic, studying computer theory. Others focus on applying their knowledge of computer science and programming to pursuing rewarding careers in an assortment of industries.

PROGRAMMER

The software that tells a computer what to do is written by programmers. Programmers write software by using a variety of programming languages, which are designed to translate instructions from a programmer into a form that the computer can understand. A programmer may work for a company that produces commercial software or a company where he or she writes software to run the company's internal computer systems. Some programmers work for companies where they write the software that runs the company's products. For instance, they might write a program that controls automated machinery at a factory or self-diagnostic software for automobiles. Each kind of computer language is best suited to specific applications, such as creating business

Software engineers employed by companies like Google, which develops different types of applications, often have the opportunity to work on a variety of projects.

programs, databases, video games, specialized scientific applications, and so on. Programmers learn certain programming languages depending in part on what type of applications they wish to write.

People who study computer programming in college learn many programming languages. However, new languages with additional capabilities are constantly being developed. Therefore, to remain desirable in the job market, a programmer must constantly update his or her skills by learning the latest programming languages. Programmers accomplish this by taking courses or using instructional books and CDs to teach themselves.

Technology giant Microsoft is a major presence at the annual Consumer Electronics Show, where technology companies unveil their brand-new products to the public.

INFORMATION TECHNOLOGY JOBS

Many people with a background in computer science and programming find a job in the field of information technology. "Information technology" refers to the use of computer hardware and software to transmit, store, and analyze information. Today, most companies have one or more information technology (IT) employees, and many companies have IT departments. The following are examples of information technology jobs.

SYSTEM OR NETWORK ADMINISTRATOR

Many companies configure their computers into networks. Often, computers in a network are also connected to a central server with which they exchange data. Special networking software is installed on the server to control the network.

Network administrators are responsible for constructing, monitoring, maintaining, and securing the company's network of computers and the software that runs on them. The network administrator needs to know a variety of software programs and must be able to customize software. Examples of software languages and programming tools used by systems and network administrators include Active Server Pages, Cognos, Java Server Pages, Microsoft Exchange, Microsoft .NET languages, Oracle, SQL Server, and VMWare.

System and network administrators use software to monitor the network for physical and capacity-related problems, control access to network resources, install security systems to protect it, keep the network software up-to-date, and back up the server so that data is not lost in the event of disaster. The systems administrator also uses software to control access to the company's databases, computerized records, servers, and other digital resources.

In addition to a formal education, network administrators often acquire professional certifications from companies that make networking hardware and software, such as Microsoft. To acquire a professional certification, the person must study material supplied by the company and pass a test that demonstrates that he or she understands how to use the product. These kinds of professional certifications often help a person when job hunting, since they demonstrate mastery of procedures necessary to keep the network running.

IT MANAGER

IT departments that employ a number of people are generally overseen by an IT manager. The IT manager has the authority to approve the decisions of lower-level employees. However, the manager is usually not involved in the day-to-day, hands-on operations of the company's computer systems. Rather, the manager's job is to oversee the work of his or her employees, make hiring and firing decisions, interact with senior management to ascertain the company's computing needs, create and monitor the departmental budget, obtain approval for necessary purchases from senior management, and perform other managerial tasks.

To be successful, an IT manager should have an education in both computer technology and business and management skills. Many people who rise up through the ranks to attain a

For anyone pursuing a career in computer science and programming, staying up-to-date on the latest technologies is crucial. Many major manufacturers of computer components offer real-world training in how to use new technology.

management position enhance their business knowledge by taking management courses.

DATABASE ADMINISTRATOR

Companies and organizations use databases to store and organize data. This data may consist of accounting records, human resources records, the outcomes of product tests and quality assurance results, customer and prospect lists, orders received and filled, inventory information, purchasing records—the list is almost endless.

EXPLORING JOB REQUIREMENTS

A good way to get an idea of both the duties and requirements for various types of computer science and programming jobs is to check out job ads. It's best to do this while still in school, before it's time to prepare for a career in earnest. Exploring these ads will provide insight into what kinds of jobs might be appealing. Beyond this, it will provide an idea of what courses are necessary to take or what skills are required to obtain a specific type of job. There are a number of Web sites that provide listings of computer-related jobs, such as Monster.com. To see what jobs are projected to be in demand in the future, and to get an idea of salary ranges, check out the U.S. Department of Labor's *Occupational Outlook Handbook* (http://www.bls.gov/oco).

The person in charge of organizing and maintaining all this information is the database administrator. One of the key responsibilities of a database administrator is designing the structure of the database. This includes figuring out what information should be kept in the database, and in what form. Database administrators must have a solid knowledge of database creation software, such as SQL or Oracle, and the ability to interact with the employees of the organization to find out what data they need to perform their jobs.

Other duties of database administrators include implementing proper security procedures to keep data secure, backing up the database so that the information is safe in case of disaster, controlling who has access to the database, using software to monitor the performance of the database so that users do not experience long wait times when trying to access data, and troubleshooting problems with database access.

CAREERS IN COMPUTER SERVICES

An alternative to working in IT is to work for a company that provides computer-related services to businesses. Such companies range from nationwide chains to one-person operations. Some computer services companies focus on selling businesses computer networks and installing them. These companies may provide the computers and peripherals, or use the equipment provided by the customer. They run the cabling, set up the network, and install the software used by the company.

Computer services companies may also offer contracts for ongoing support of the network. In such cases, computer professionals respond to calls from the client when there is a problem with the computer network, and they travel to the client's location to fix the problem. Other computer services companies write custom software or modify commercial software to meet a company's specific needs.

Working for a computer services company requires excellent people skills as well as extensive technical knowledge. One may have to explain complex technological topics to people with little or no technical knowledge. Patience and tact are required to deal with customers who are stressed out because their computer system is having a problem.

CHAPTER 3
Preparing for a Career

Many colleges and universities today offer programs in computer science and programming. Colleges offer four-year bachelor's degree programs or two-year associate's degree programs that are suitable for entry-level jobs. Some colleges offer both full-time and part-time higher-degree programs. Technical schools are much like other colleges, except they offer programs that train students for specific jobs in the field. For example, a program at a technical school might train students on how to repair computers in order to prepare them for a career as a computer technician, or teach them how to design and build Web pages. The aspect of computer science a person wishes to work in will affect the academic courses he or she takes.

CHOOSING A FOCUS

When determining what aspect of computer science to pursue, it is necessary to decide what kind of careers seem as though they would be interesting. Computer science graduates most commonly become programmers or work in IT as systems or network administrators. Many also end up working with computer hardware. It's also important to decide what industries might be rewarding to work in. Some people are more interested in computer theory and working with others to create cutting-edge software programs. Others might be more interested in working on programming industrial robots and industrial automation processes. Still others might be most interested in using their knowledge of computer science and programming to ultimately obtain an IT management job. It is generally necessary for aspiring computer scientists, programmers, and other computer professionals to have a basic grounding in both computer hardware and software. Computer scientists and programmers might work in a number of different industries before deciding on which one they enjoy the most.

The Association of Computing Machinery (ACM), a large computer industry organization, has defined a

These high school students are learning about programming in the school's computer lab. Computer classes can help students get a head start in learning how to code.

number of general areas of academic study in computer science and programming. The following is a list of some of the major areas of academic study in which degrees are offered. The exact title of a degree will vary from institution to institution.

- **Computer Science:** This is a broad category in which a student learns about computer hardware technology and programming. Some programs of study focus on the theoretical side of computer science, while others focus more on programming. Students learning about computer science will study a wide range of computer hardware and software subjects. People with computer science degrees are often qualified to work in a wide range of fields.

- **Computer Engineering:** This area of study combines the study of computer science with electrical engineering. It provides students with the skills to design computer systems and computerized devices. Some of the areas listed by the ACM in which graduates may design devices include consumer electronics, medical device development, military technology, security systems, and telecommunications.

- **Programming:** Programming, or software engineering, emphasizes the creation of programs to run computerized applications. This is accomplished by using various kinds of programming languages. Examples from the ACM include developing software to run "avionics, health care applications, cryptography, traffic control, meteorological systems and the like."

CAREER PREPARATION

It's never too soon to begin preparing for a career in computer science or programming. If it is possible to take a computer class at school, then by all means take it. Not only can these classes provide useful skills, but they can also provide students with an opportunity to learn whether they find working with computers to be interesting and fulfilling.

It is easy to look at cool applications on a computer or an iPhone and want to create some. It's another thing to understand the math and science that are used behind the scenes to create an application. College-level computer science and programming curriculums will contain a great number of math and science courses. Therefore, it's important to get as thorough a grounding as possible in math and science while still in high school. It is necessary to take courses in algebra and precalculus, as well as calculus if it is offered. Calculus forms the basis of computer algorithms, which are a set of steps used to accomplish a task or solve a problem.

People pursuing a career in computer science or programming will need to take courses in statistics, which are used in data analysis, in high school or college. Physics courses can help students understand the principles that underlie electronics. In addition to academic courses, students should join their high school's computer club and work on learning practical computer skills. Volunteering in the school's computer lab is another way to gain some hands-on computer knowledge.

BUILDING SKILLS FOR SUCCESS

Junior high and high school students should not only be focused on learning how to be computer experts. At this time, it's important to learn the basic skills that are crucial to being successful. For instance, it's good for aspiring computer professionals to take a typing course. Whether working with hardware or software, computer scientists and programmers spend a lot of time typing at the keyboard. Knowing how to touch-type speeds up work immensely. Above all, it is necessary to learn good written and spoken communication skills. Every major position in computer science and programming today, whether it is in IT, data analysis, or software design, involves interacting with both rank-and-file employees and managers. In addition, it's rare for computer systems and software to be developed by a single individual. Instead, this work is done by a team. Therefore, it is necessary to be able to communicate ideas both in writing and verbally to coworkers and superiors. Having good communication skills can ensure that one's ideas are conveyed in a clear and direct manner.

STUDYING COMPUTER SCIENCE IN COLLEGE

Students who go to college for computer science and programming will likely pursue a course of study incorporating a diverse selection of classes. These can include courses in mathematics and the natural sciences. They will also take general courses in computer science, which can include introduction to computer systems, introduction to data structures, programming courses in specific languages such as C and Unix, and computational mathematics. General computer science courses can be applied to any career in computer technology.

Students can also take courses in specific areas of computer science that interest them, such as multimedia, robotics, computer graphics, and artificial intelligence (developing computer systems that can learn and make decisions). Students will most likely take mathematics courses such as advanced calculus and algebra, as well as statistics and probability, which are used to analyze the likelihood of various events occurring. They can also expect to take courses in the

Mathematics and logic are the foundation of computer programming. An understanding of these subjects is key to the creation of algorithms, which govern how programs run.

natural sciences, such as physics, and basic courses in engineering and experimental design. Becoming knowledgeable in experimental design is key to being able to design technology projects.

Students may also take courses in ethical computing, particularly on how to maintain the confidentiality of data and protect people's privacy. Students will most likely do work in a computer lab, where they will perform computer-related tasks and write programs. Thus, they will be expected to demonstrate hands-on knowledge of the material they cover. In addition to technical courses, students may be expected to take a variety of electives in the humanities and arts.

Some colleges offer courses in communication and business for engineers, which can prove to be extremely useful. To be successful in the real world, it is necessary to understand more than computer technology. Aspiring computer scientists and programmers need to have solid communication, project management, and people management skills. A person who understands how to manage people and projects is more valuable to a company than one who only knows how a computer operates. In fact, most computer science and programming jobs today require basic management skills, such as the ability to create a budget and justify expenditures. For these reasons, students may want to take some basic courses in business management, project management, and finance.

Finally, one of the simplest and most useful things a college student can do is to practice good work habits. Completing work in a thorough and timely fashion in college creates work habits that will advance a student's career once he or she enters the workforce.

THE ADVANTAGES OF A BROAD EDUCATION

In today's world of business and industry, people from all backgrounds work together. It's not unusual for computer scientists and programmers to find themselves working for companies with branches in more than one country, serving customers from around the world. A computer professional may very well find himself or herself working with people from other countries and at some point traveling to work sites abroad. For this reason, it is beneficial to have a background in areas outside

Many people in the field of computer science find themselves working internationally. Here, a computer professional works on a project at a major computer company in Beijing, China.

the realm of technology. Taking college courses in history, philosophy, and psychology can be very beneficial in gaining an understanding of the world in general and how people interact. This kind of background can enhance a person's knowledge of, and tolerance for, the diverse cultures and beliefs of people he or she may encounter in a professional capacity.

It is also possible to combine the study of computer technology science and programming with other fields of study. In almost every field today, there is tremendous demand for employees who are knowledgeable about the use of computers and software. Therefore, even if a student doesn't wish to become a professional computer scientist per se, he or she may wish to learn certain aspects of computer hardware or programming. Having skills in these areas can make a person more competitive in the job marketplace and more valuable as an employee. For this reason, those who are interested in pursuing jobs in a wide variety of industries, such as scientific research, medical technology, business, industrial production, energy, or telecommunications, may want to take courses in computer science in addition to their main course of study.

Today's employers are often looking to hire employees with a broad range of skills. Not only is there an increasingly large overlap between many areas of knowledge used in business and industry today, but the technology used throughout the professional world is changing at a rapid pace. Employees who can demonstrate that they are able to adapt to new kinds of technology will have a leg up on those who can't. Employers are interested in hiring people who not only are familiar with the technological tools in their field, but also have a broad base of communication skills, knowledge of the liberal arts, and scientific knowledge. The most valuable employees are those who not only understand technology but also the business of the company they work for, and those who can represent the company well to management, customers, suppliers, and business partners. Having this kind of combined knowledge can enable a job seeker to present himself or herself as a formidable candidate for a job.

TYPES OF SCHOOLS AND PROGRAMS

Getting a college degree in computer science is the most effective way to prepare for a long-term career in the field. A formal education trains a person in a broad range of technologies and techniques, better equipping him or her to meet the demands of the workplace. By providing knowledge of the theoretical underpinnings of computers, it allows a person to understand how new technologies work. College coursework can train people in how to effectively approach projects and problem solving in general. Having this training makes an aspiring computer professional more successful at solving problems and dealing with issues when working in the real world. Getting a degree also demonstrates to an employer that the person can successfully pursue a goal to completion. Higher-level IT positions are easier to obtain with a degree.

Technical schools generally offer both four-year bachelor's degree programs and two-year associate's degree programs. Associate's degree programs concentrate on particular technical skills, such as computer network administration and software development. They are designed to prepare students for entry-level positions working with computer hardware

Technical schools, such as ITT Technical Institute in Anaheim, California, provide students with a practical education in computer science that allows them to get started on a career.

and software. In many cases, if a person with an associate's degree wishes to continue with his or her education in a four-year bachelor's degree program, it is possible to get credit for courses already taken. In the field of computer science and programming, students can get degrees in computer science, software applications development, computer systems security, electronics and communications technology, and electrical engineering, among others.

Many institutions that have degree programs in computer science also offer certificate programs. Certificate programs are designed primarily for working professionals who wish to expand their knowledge of computer science or programming. This is especially true of those who need to familiarize themselves with new technologies—for example, programming for mobile computing or cyber security (using computer-based security systems to ensure the safety of people, objects, and buildings). Certificate programs usually take one or two years to complete and are often offered part-time.

Although a college graduate might start out doing basic computer technology or programming tasks for which hands-on experience is sufficient, the higher that person rises in a company, the more important it is that he or she have the kind of broad knowledge base that can be gained through a formal education. Those interested in pursuing careers in areas such as designing new computers and electronic devices, or pursuing research in areas such as artificial intelligence, robotics, and other cutting-edge technologies, would do well to seek higher levels of education. Beyond bachelor's degree programs in their computer science departments, many colleges also offer master's degree and Ph.D. programs.

INTERNSHIPS

One of the greatest challenges faced by new job seekers is that they often must compete against more experienced candidates. Previous experience demonstrates to employers that a person can perform the tasks the job requires, whereas a person who is just starting out and has no previous experience is an unknown quantity to an employer. So how does a person gain experience while still in school? One way is by getting an internship. Internships are unpaid positions that give a student the chance to learn on-the-job skills. Interns perform basic tasks while observing professionals in the field at work.

SCHOLARSHIPS AND GRANTS

Students interested in pursuing an education in computer science may want to check out scholarships and grants that can help cover the cost. The International Society of Electrical and Electronics Engineers maintains a special student Web site (http://www.ieeeusa.org/careers/student.menu.html) that, among other things, contains links to information on scholarships, grants, and technical contests open to students attending college. The American Society for Engineering Education maintains a "Student Blog" Web site (http://students.egfi-k12.org) for students in elementary, middle, and high school. Among other information, it provides a list of organizations offering scholarships for students interested in studying technology and engineering.

Internships allow students to gain hands-on experience working with computers, computer networks, and software. They provide an opportunity for interns to see how the tools and techniques they learned in college are applied in the real world. Interns can also gain invaluable experience in how computer and software projects are carried out in a professional setting. If students do a good job as interns, their employers may provide references that they can use when they are looking for a job. In addition, an intern's coworkers can be valuable contacts when he or she is ready to enter the workforce.

Some colleges offer programs that include a semester of practical internship. Students interested in taking advantage of additional opportunities can also check out the Association of Computing Machinery's Crossroads Internship Database on its Web site. This resource lists specific companies that offer internships and provides links to general resources where employers advertise internships. The International Society of Electrical and Electronics Engineers (IEEE), another major technology and engineering society, offers a number of summer and temporary internships through its student Web site. Another resource is the American Society for Engineering Education (ASEE) Tech Intern Web site.

CHAPTER 4

Getting Involved and Gaining Exposure

In today's competitive job market, it's beneficial to gain experience and exposure before starting to look for a job. There are a number of different ways to meet other people in the field and develop a portfolio of work while still in college or even in high school. Being involved in the larger community of computer professionals and software developers provides several benefits. It offers a chance to learn about the field by talking with experienced professionals. In addition, it provides the chance to apply the skills learned in the classroom to real-life projects and the chance to learn proper professional behavior from those who already work in the field.

BUILDING A PORTFOLIO OF WORK

The best way for a job applicant to demonstrate to a prospective employer that he or she is qualified for the job is to create a portfolio. A portfolio is a collection of work samples. For instance, a programmer's portfolio would contain examples of his or her programming work.

Even if a person hasn't done any professional work yet, it's still possible to create work for a portfolio. One way to do this is to build apps. Popular social media sites such as Facebook and Twitter support apps, and people can practice

APPS

What's an app? It's a short form of the word "application." Apps are often small programs that serve a single function—for instance, a simple game or puzzle, or a poll in which people vote on a particular topic. Smartphones such as the Apple iPhone feature thousands of downloadable apps, many of which were designed and built by users.

A person interested in a programming career can showcase his or her abilities by creating apps. Apple provides an interface that individuals can use to develop apps for the iPhone, a highly popular activity for both amateur and professional programmers. (In fact, designing iPhone apps is so popular that Stanford University in California offers a special course in it.) Although the apps need to be approved by Apple before they can be distributed through Apple's App Store, simply developing an app provides a handy example of one's work.

Smartphones like the Google Nexus One (left) and Apple iPhone (right) have created an enormous market for apps.

their basic programming skills by creating simple apps for their page. Some students also create mods, or add-ons for popular video games. Mods can add additional levels, maps, or other elements to a game. Many game manufacturers provide toolkits to people interested in creating mods. Web sites for popular games often feature information on mods and modding. Students should take advantage of every opportunity to create programs or applications that show their skills and include them in their portfolios.

BECOMING PART OF THE OPEN SOURCE COMMUNITY

Another way to develop credentials in the computer science and programming field is to participate in the open source software community. This community is a collection of people who are interested in creating and sharing open source software. There are two basic categories of software: proprietary and open source. Proprietary software is copyrighted by the individual or the company that created it. For example, Microsoft software products, such as Microsoft Word, are proprietary. Proprietary software may not be used without paying a license fee or having the explicit permission of the copyright owner. Open source software, in contrast, is made available to be used by anyone, free of charge, by the person or organization that creates it.

There may be some limitations associated with the right to use open source software, such as agreeing that anything created with it must also be open source. But it can be used,

Oracle CEO Larry Ellison gives the keynote address at Oracle OpenWorld in 2006. This conference brings computer users, innovators, professionals, and business leaders together.

enhanced, or modified by anyone at will. An example of an open source resource is the online encyclopedia Wikipedia. Anyone can contribute to Wikipedia, or review and edit existing entries. Open source software is much the same—programmers can modify the source code to improve or otherwise change the software.

The most well-known example of open source software is Linux. A version of Unix operating system software that was originally developed by Linus Torvalds, Linux is one of the most widely used operating systems in business and industry today. Individuals all over the world work on enhancing open

KEEPING UP WITH THE FIELD

Innovations in the world of computer hardware and software happen constantly. Brand-new cutting-edge technologies, devices, and programming languages are continually being developed. New versions of existing products with different applications and features come out every year. For this reason, it is critical that computer scientists and programmers keep up with the field. They need to stay up-to-date with the most current books, trade magazines, and online articles. Being active in professional organizations such as the IEEE, ASEE, or ACM is an excellent way for them to not only stay up to date with the new technologies being developed, but to sometimes even play a role in their development.

It is important to understand that computer science and programming is not a field where a person can get a degree, put his or her books away, and proceed to have a lifelong career. If computer professionals do not continually update their knowledge, they will inevitably become obsolete, just like the programming languages and computer technology they learned at the start of their career. A career in computer science means a lifelong commitment to learning.

source software, and new versions and applications for use with it are continually emerging.

Open source software exists for audio and video applications, business productivity, databases, math and science applications, software development, security, video games, and more. Many of the major open source programs such as Ubuntu (an open source alternative to the Windows operating system) and the Firefox Web browser maintain links on their sites to developers' forums for those interested in participating in development and support.

Individuals belonging to the open source community work on open source software projects alone or in groups, communicating with other members of the community via online forums devoted to a particular type of software. Online forums allow users to exchange ideas and help each other with questions and problems. Individual utilities and applications that can be used with the existing version of a program are often offered, free of charge, to the open source community by the person who created them.

Another way to participate in the software community at large is through problem-solving forums. Almost every major manufacturer of software hosts community forums where users help each other resolve problems with commercial software, such as Windows or Adobe Flash. The same is true of some major online sites, such as YouTube, which host community help forums. In these forums, participants can use their knowledge to help others resolve problems.

Participating in the larger community of programmers can provide a person with the opportunity to practice his or her software skills by working on real-world applications. Being part of a community also allows a person to get to know other professionals working in the areas he or she is interested in and gain recognition as someone who contributes to the community. Some organizations and companies even recognize individuals who make a significant contribution to helping others with their software. For example, Microsoft grants the Microsoft Most Valuable Player award to those who make a significant contribution to supporting their Microsoft software through technical forums.

PARTICIPATING IN PROFESSIONAL ASSOCIATIONS

Organizations such as the ACM and IEEE offer student memberships. Joining and participating in the activities of such an organization is a great way to demonstrate an interest in the field. Through its partnership with major software manufacturers, such as Microsoft Corporation and Sun Microsystems, the ACM can offer its student members access to more than one hundred software programs. These programs provide an enormous variety of tools for learning and building sample computer applications. The ACM even has a special newsletter for students.

In addition, being a student member of an organization like the ACM or IEEE provides the opportunity to learn about various subdisciplines of the field. If a student wishes to work on a computer science or programming project, he or she will have expert contacts who can give advice. Further, students will be making contacts with professionals in the field who may be able to help them when it comes time to look for internships or employment. The IEEE maintains a student Web site that provides information on opportunities of special interest to students.

The ACM offers twenty stipends of $500 each to allow students to attend research conferences in computer science. Although these stipends are mostly aimed at college students, high school students are eligible to apply. If they can demonstrate sufficient interest in research and study in the field, they can qualify.

CHAPTER 5

Finding a Job

At one time, people checked the newspaper want ads when they wanted to look for a job. Today, most companies in the software and computer industries rely on online, rather than print, advertising. Generally, only a small portion of available jobs are listed in newspaper ads. Simply looking through print ads is often the least effective way to find a job; the job seeker should look through other employment resources as well.

Larger companies often use recruitment agencies, sometimes called "head hunters," to locate employees. This is especially true for technical and managerial positions. One can look up recruitment agencies in the phone book or do a Yellow Pages search on a search engine such as Yahoo! or Google. However, the chances of getting a job through a recruitment agency are greater once a person has experience in the field.

JOB SEARCH STRATEGIES

Many colleges and technical schools have a placement office that assists students with finding a job. In addition to helping students contact companies, the placement office often provides resources for writing résumés and other job hunting tools. Many professional organizations have job hunting resources for their members, including online resources and newsletters that list job opportunities.

The first step to finding a good job is setting a concrete goal to aim for. It's one thing to want to have a career in computer science or programming, but another to have a specific career path in mind. When beginning the process of job searching, identify companies that seem interesting or look like good places to work. These can be found by looking through an online industry directory, printed directories provided by industry associations, or general business directories such as Standard & Poor's or the Dow Jones directories, which are available at many libraries.

PREPARING A RÉSUMÉ

The most important tool for job hunting is a résumé. A résumé is a document that lists the applicant's educational background, work experience, and other pertinent information. For instance, a job applicant might list the internships he or she completed on a résumé. The purpose of a résumé is to get an interview with prospective employers. Therefore, it should include information that shows that the applicant has skills not only in computer science and programming, but also in other areas that will make him or her a valuable candidate for the job.

When crafting a résumé, it's best to steer clear of trendy or unusual formats that might affect the résumé's readability. Complicated designs can make it more difficult for an employer to locate information such as what jobs an applicant has held. Faced with going through enormous numbers of résumés in response to a job posting, employers are not likely to spend time hunting through a résumé for the information they want to know.

Applicants shouldn't limit themselves to simply listing technical skills. They should think about the company's industry and the job they are applying for. What nontechnical skills might a potential employer be looking for? Applicants should list skills or experience in areas such as sales, negotiating, running meetings, preparing multimedia presentations, and budget creation on their résumés.

Applicants should be sure to not only list their job responsibilities and duties when creating a résumé, but also detail their accomplishments. For example, a résumé might include information such as: "Built pilot system to help train university lab staff and demonstrate feasibility of using the AVVID product to fulfill the university's needs," or "Upgraded Big Brother/Big Sister computer system so that students would have access to streaming video to enhance effectiveness of after-school learning program." When writing a résumé, the sentences describing the applicant's accomplishments should be simple and direct, without excess words that might detract from the main point. Potential employers should understand that the applicant not only has technical skills, but also has a history of using these skills to accomplish projects.

Applicants shouldn't include irrelevant personal information on their résumés, but including relevant personal information can help an employer get a better idea of the applicant. For example, if a job applicant has previously volunteered with an environmental organization such as Greenpeace or the Sierra Club, he or she should mention that when applying for a job with a company working in alternative energy technology. Applicants who have honed their skills by donating their time and expertise to charitable organizations should mention that on their résumés. Many companies are increasingly interested in playing a meaningful role in their communities, and volunteering shows that an applicant is the kind of person who is willing to help others.

Résumés should always be focused on specific jobs. We live in an age when the Internet provides easy access to information, so there is no excuse for applicants to not research the company they are applying to. Likewise, it's easy to customize a résumé on the computer so that it states one is applying for the specific job a company is trying to fill and highlights the skills being advertised for, such as knowledge of particular programming languages or technologies.

Above all else, applicants should make sure that their résumé is neat, professional looking, and thoroughly proofread so that it does not contain mistakes. No company wants to hire a sloppy programmer.

NETWORKING

The most successful way to find a job is often through networking with other people, rather than simply looking online or in print ads. When networking, a person can contact people he or she knows in the field and ask them for assistance in locating a job. The majority of jobs are filled before they ever get listed in the newspaper or online. This is where developing contacts through interning, participating in the open source community and in problem-solving forums, and joining industry organizations can help get the word out that a person is looking for a job. When networking, be sure to get people's contact information. This includes their name, e-mail address, and (if meeting someone in person) their business card. This way, they can be contacted during the

The MacWorld convention, seen here in 2009, is held annually by Apple to showcase the company's latest products, as well as applications and products by other vendors.

job hunting process. Even if they don't know of a job opening, they may be able to provide the names of people who can help.

PRESENTING A PORTFOLIO

Regardless of how an applicant locates job leads, experts agree that, in today's competitive job market, having a portfolio of work to show potential employers is key to getting a job interview. As students work on projects in school or during summer jobs and internships, they should be sure to assemble examples of the work they have done.

The latest trend in job hunting is the construction of electronic portfolios. Many people are now maintaining electronic portfolios online to assist potential employers in evaluating them. An electronic portfolio contains examples of a person's work, which prospective employers can view, along with a copy of the person's résumé. A person can also include a sample of Web pages or applications on a CD or DVD in his or her portfolio. A résumé, along with a top-notch demo of a person's work, can help an applicant land a job. Remember that any work presented in a portfolio must be of the best quality one is capable of producing.

WHERE TO LOOK FOR WORK

A vast number of computer science and programming jobs exist in a wide range of industries. All these industries need computer scientists and programmers to build and maintain computer systems.

BUSINESS AND MANUFACTURING

Computers and software are found everywhere in businesses. Accounting is done on computer systems for large and small businesses. Businesses use databases to maintain records, and keep track of sales and marketing information, such as data on clients. Databases are also used to analyze data about potential customers, target those most likely to buy the company's products, and analyze the results of advertising campaigns.

Many manufacturing businesses rely on database systems for inventory management. They track the receipt of goods and keep track of stock levels so that items can be reordered before supplies run out. Purchasing systems keep track of orders and match received goods to purchase orders. Sales systems are used to keep track of orders for finished products and shipping information.

Programmers are often required to write custom database programs for businesses. These custom databases are designed to record the particular types of information a company needs to keep track of and analyze. In addition, programmers often have to write custom software that will integrate various types of software used by a company. For example, a company may need to exchange information between its order entry, finance, and sales and marketing departments. In this case, it would be necessary for a programmer to write software that converts each system's data into a form that can be understood by the other systems. A programmer might come up with a way to have the inventory and purchasing systems "talk" to each other so that parts can automatically be reordered when the inventory level drops to a predefined point.

Computer systems are used to control many manufacturing processes. Nearly all of today's factory production lines are automated, or run by computers that control the machines creating the final product. Programmers are needed to write machine automation software for companies that manufacture automated equipment. They are also needed to write, alter, and maintain custom software that runs particular processes in a given manufacturing facility. There are a variety of computer science–related jobs on both the business and manufacturing sides of industry.

TRANSPORTATION

Computers are used in every phase of transportation today. They are used by air traffic controllers to manage air flights and in aircraft to control the flight systems themselves. Programmers write the code used in trucks and trains to relay information about the location of vehicles and their cargo, allowing companies to track the progress of shipments and drivers. Programmers write code used by governments to monitor traffic patterns and assess issues related to traffic control. They also write code to model future transportation systems. For example, these programs might model traffic patterns to establish what the best design for proposed highway systems would be. In addition, vehicle manufacturers employ computer science experts to develop the electronic components and code that control vehicles.

Beyond earthbound transportation, programmers write the code used in aerospace applications to control spacecraft, such as space shuttles and operate satellites, and provide data-gathering and analysis functions at NASA.

A scientist at NASA who works on the Mars Rover team explains how images and data collected by NASA's Spirit rover are used to create a virtual model of the red planet's landscape.

SECURITY

One of the fastest-growing areas of employment today is in security systems. Concerns about crime and terrorism have fueled an ever-increasing demand for integrated security systems. Integrated systems connect various devices to create a single system that performs a complex function, such as providing security. An integrated security system might combine security elements such as video cameras and alarms with sophisticated computers that control the overall security system, store data, and then analyze it. These systems often include elements such as card key locks that record data on who enters specific areas and when. Programmers are required to write the programs that run and integrate these systems. They write special computer security programs, including biometric programs such as facial recognition software. They also help create large databases that store information on dangerous people, such as known terrorists or criminals. Three types of security companies provide employment to programmers: the companies that manufacture the systems, the companies that maintain the systems and staff them, and the agencies that use such systems.

ENERGY

Computers control the flow of electrical energy that keeps modern society operating. Vast computer systems control the operation of power plants and the distribution of power throughout electrical grids. All those systems must be networked and programmed. Programmers also create software that operates advanced alternative energy systems, such as

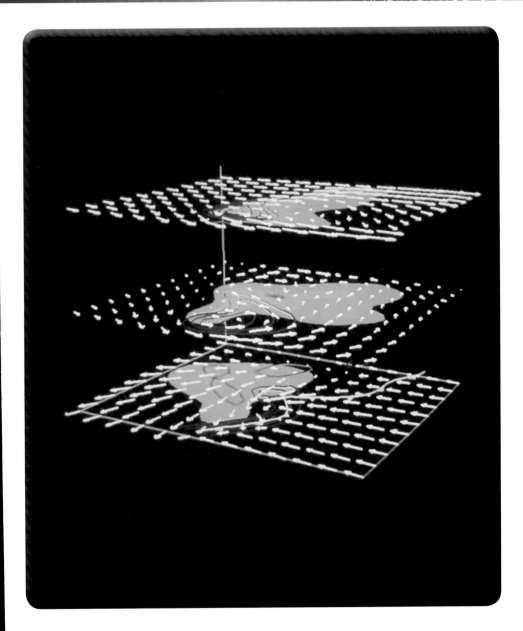

This computer model of a thunderstorm with a tornado brewing was constructed from Doppler radar data.

arrays of photovoltaic panels that convert sunlight into electrical energy.

MEDICINE

Computers have become a central part of medical technology. For a long time, they have been used to keep track of patient records. But soon there will be centralized medical databases that will keep track of patients' medical information, such as tests, prescriptions, diseases, and the like. This system will enable doctors, nurses, and other medical professionals to easily access a patient's medical information. Keeping all patient information in one place could streamline medical treatment and reduce the cost of doing repeated tests. The need to create and maintain these medical systems will create many programming jobs in the coming years, both in hospitals and with companies that will provide the software for this purpose.

Systems are also being developed that assist medical personnel in identifying and diagnosing medical problems. These systems work by analyzing symptoms entered into a computer. The system then suggests possible medical problems indicated by the symptoms and recommends appropriate tests. Such systems rely on "knowledge bases." These are large collections of data that consist of information obtained from experts in a particular field. The building of knowledge bases is, in itself, another type of programming job.

SCIENCE

Today, every type of science relies heavily on computers. Two major applications of computer systems in such areas

A computer professional runs a simulation of an unmanned aerial vehicle (UAV) during a 2009 meeting of the Association for Unmanned Vehicle System International.

are mapping and modeling, both of which require programming. Mapping involves taking data from sensors on vehicles, such as planes or ships, downloading it to computers, and then creating maps. For instance, video cameras mounted on aircraft might take pictures of terrain, and these images could be downloaded to land-based computers, which would create a map of how much forest exists in a certain area. Pictures from satellites orbiting Earth could be analyzed to determine the health of Earth's ozone layer. Maps can be created that show the distribution of different types of terrain or the location of oil deposits.

Modeling uses computers and software to predict what might happen under certain conditions. Modeling is used to predict weather events such as hurricanes and tornadoes, as well as predict the effects of human activities on global warming. It is used in designing industrial products by creating "virtual" objects, such as the components of an engine, to see how the final product might run before investing money in building a prototype, or trial version. It is used by biotechnology and pharmaceutical companies to evaluate how new drugs might work before testing them in the real world. Programmers are often hired to create commercial mapping and modeling software and to customize programs for specific projects being undertaken by research organizations.

THE MILITARY

Programmers are needed to write programs for a wide range of military applications. The military uses computers in communication systems, to operate remote "drones" (unmanned vehicles that provide information on the location of enemy troops and facilities), in advanced weapons systems such as missile guidance systems, and in engineering applications, among other things. The military is not a career choice for everyone, especially when the country is at war. However, many people use their interest in computer science and programming to engage in a technical career and serve their country at the same time. People who choose this career path may qualify to receive computer training through the military.

CHAPTER 6

What to Expect on the Job

What a computer professional's work experience will be like will depend on both the industry and the size of the company where he or she chooses to work. Some people prefer to work for large corporations, which often provide higher-paying jobs and more benefits, such as health insurance and tuition reimbursement, than smaller companies. However, it can be harder to be noticed at a large company, and one's responsibilities may be more limited than they might be at a small company. Rules and procedures are also likely to be more formally defined at large companies.

Many people are more comfortable working for small companies, which often provide more flexible working hours and have a less formal work environment. In addition, the camaraderie among the members of a small staff working together to create new projects is often much greater than at a workplace with a large staff. However, salaries are likely to be lower than they would be at a larger company, and smaller companies may provide their employees with fewer benefits. On the other hand, small companies sometimes provide stock to employees. This stock may be provided in lieu of some part of one's salary or offered when the company starts to sell stock to the public. Large companies such as eBay, Microsoft, and Apple all started out as small companies with few employees. For those who like structure, the work environment at a small company may seem chaotic or unstable. Although large companies are less likely than small companies to go out of business in bad economic times, an employee could still be laid off if the company's business takes a turn for the worse.

Some people prefer to work for themselves, freelancing. This approach lacks the security of a regular paycheck, but it offers freelancers the opportunity to work on a variety of projects with many different types of companies. Freelancing can also provide a larger income, since a freelancer or consultant is not limited to a set salary.

A person's choice of industry also influences his or her working environment. There will obviously be a difference in the atmosphere of the workplace if one works for the military, a power plant, or an intelligence agency, compared to an alternative energy company, a charity, or a company developing a video game. It's important for aspiring computer professionals to thoroughly consider what type of environment they would be happy working in.

Also, it's important to consider personal interests. Because the use of computer technology is so widespread and the variety of positions is so large, it is not difficult to combine an interest in another area, such as art, medicine, science, or entertainment, with a computer science or programming career. For instance, if a person loves art, he or she can look for a job programming software applications that create computer graphics or animation. Those interested in music or film can look for companies that offer positions in these areas or are involved in broadcasting. If one is interested in a science such as geology or ecology, one can look for firms doing analysis in these areas. The possibilities are endless.

Although a huge variety of different jobs exist in the field of computer science and programming, these examples will provide some idea of what it's like working in both the hardware and software sides of the field.

WORKING AS A PROGRAMMER

Programmers may work alone or with others. A single programmer might create a small program or modify an existing one. It is more common, however, for programmers to work together. Large applications are created by a team of programmers. When programmers work together as a team, they divide the work up amongst themselves. For instance, each programmer in the team might work on a specific part, or module, of the overall program.

Before any program can be written, it is necessary to find out what the program's users will need it to do. This is called requirements gathering. At this stage, programmers meet with management and potential users of the product to find out what functionality they want the program to have. They figure out how users are going to interact with the program. Good observation skills and good listening skills are required.

It's not enough to write a program that performs a task. The program must perform the task in a way that is natural and comfortable for users. Therefore, before any code is written, the programmer draws up a design for what the program will do and how it will work. Often, he or she makes mockups of screens and reviews them with users and managers. The programmer must get management's approval of the design, as well as the budget for the project, before beginning work.

Programmers often present several different ideas for the program to management, which selects one.

Programming projects are sometimes run by a project manager—an individual whose job it is to keep track of the progress of the project. Project managers also keep track of the project's costs as they are incurred. This is done in order to ensure that the project stays on budget and on schedule. Programmers and project managers often use special project management software to track these aspects of the project.

Once a project is approved, the programmer will spend most of his or her time writing code. This is a cyclical process. The programmer writes code, then runs it on test computers to see if it works the way it's supposed to. New software often contains errors, called bugs. Running the software reveals the bugs, which can then be corrected by the programmer. Bugs are generally recorded in a log, along with information on how they were corrected. This way, if the same bug occurs in the future, the programmers will know how to fix it. Once the bug is fixed, the program is run again. This process is repeated until the program runs without generating errors. The program is then installed on company computers, where it can be accessed by users. The programmer may be involved in teaching users how to use the program.

In addition to writing new programs, programmers may be asked to write small programs that can expand the capabilities of existing systems or enable them to exchange data with new systems acquired by the company. They may also be asked to write "patches" to fix problems discovered after the software is installed.

Programmers can apply their programming skills to other areas of employment as well. For instance, they can go on to

This 1979 photo shows Apple cofounder Steve Jobs with the Apple II computer. Today, Apple employs more than thirty-four thousand people worldwide and the company is worth $230 billion.

become software architects, who design large software projects; management information system managers, who run departments that analyze large amounts of data and generate reports with information required by management to run the company; or project managers.

WORKING AS A SYSTEMS OR NETWORK ADMINISTRATOR

The systems or network administrator's most important job is to keep the company's computer systems running so that users can do their jobs. This involves both short-term and long-term tasks, both of which the administrator will deal with in the course of a typical day.

Long-term tasks can include backing up the system's data so that it is safe in case of computer failure or disaster, upgrading the software programs that run on the company's computers so that they stay current, and continually upgrading security software to protect the system. Administrators must also monitor the servers that run services for users and store database information to ensure that they are performing at a fast enough speed for users to work efficiently.

In order to keep track of when different tasks need to be accomplished, the administrator needs to be highly organized and keep detailed records of all the software and hardware in use in the company. To monitor how the computer systems are functioning, administrators use software that shows statistics on the utilization of system components.

Systems or network administrators also have to constantly deal with short-term demands and problems. The

THE WORLD OF FREELANCING

Many people who study computer science in college go on to pursue rewarding careers as freelancers, providing services directly to clients. They may repair computers, create computer networks, or work on teams writing custom software programs for a particular project. Freelancers can schedule their time as they wish, act as their own boss, and earn an income based on their ability to attract clients. Having this kind of freedom is very attractive to people who pursue careers as freelancers; however, with this freedom comes great responsibility. Freelancers must also control their expenses to ensure that they make a profit, they generally work alone and lack the sustained professional and social contact of a workplace, they must do a significant amount of marketing of their services to obtain clients, they must pay for their own benefits (such as health and dental insurance), and they must have enough money to live on until they build up a client base. It is also important that freelancers stick to project schedules and finish work in a timely manner. Building a reputation as a dependable worker can allow freelancers to get work through word-of-mouth recommendations. People who are interested in pursuing a career in computer science and programming as a freelancer can benefit greatly from taking college courses in business and finance in addition to computer courses.

administrator is in charge of assigning security permissions to users to allow them to access certain computers, software, or databases. For example, only human resources personnel might be allowed to access employee records, and only the finance department staff and senior management might be allowed to access the company's financial records. In a typical day, a systems or network administrator may be asked to create an account in the system for a new employee, block access for an employee who's left the company, fix a problem for a manager who is having trouble accessing the system, and set up a new smartphone for a salesperson.

Administrators also have the usual managerial responsibilities for making and tracking budgets, getting approval from senior management for new equipment and software, and then evaluating, ordering, and installing it. In medium and large companies, system and network administrators may also have employees working for them, whom they need to supervise. It is not unusual for system and network administrators to be "on call" when away from work. Being on call means they can be called to come in to the company at any time to deal with an emergency, such as the company's Web server ceasing to work. Pay for systems and network administrators is generally high, but the job can be very demanding. The career path for systems and network administrators often leads to becoming an information technology manager and could ultimately lead to becoming a vice president of IT or even chief information officer, a senior management position responsible for overseeing all of a corporation's information technology functions worldwide.

BEING A PROFESSIONAL

We've all enjoyed films and TV shows where a computer programmer in torn jeans and dirty T-shirt saves the world by hacking a computer system. However, in the real world,

When working on-site, it is important to maintain a professional demeanor with clients, even when problems are hard to diagnose and people are difficult to deal with.

companies are more likely to respect—and promote—employees who look and act professional. What constitutes appropriate dress varies among computer professionals, depending on the nature of the company, the industry, and the position held.

Those working for large companies and in positions where they come in contact with customers will most likely be expected to wear dress slacks with a shirt and tie if they are male, or an appropriate dress, skirt and jacket, or pants suit if they are female. For programmers who work strictly behind the scenes, a decent pair of slacks and shirt or sweater is likely to be acceptable. However, if a person's job involves contact with managers, especially senior managers, it's crucial that he or she be well-dressed. If management admires an employee's technical skill and thinks the employee is presentable, he or she is more likely to be considered for a more responsible position. Small companies, especially those with only a few employees, are often more flexible in how they expect employees to dress. If an employee dresses casually on the job in such a firm, however, he or she needs to be aware of when customers, representatives from larger companies interested in working jointly with theirs, or even potential investors may be visiting in order to dress appropriately and make a professional impression.

What's not open to debate is the need to treat everyone around one professionally and with respect: managers, customers, coworkers, subordinates—whomever one comes in contact with. Employees should behave honestly and responsibly on the job, and show up on time and get their part of the work done on schedule. They should demonstrate that they can manage themselves and their work. If management sees an employee as reliable, they are more likely to advance that person to a position where he or she has greater responsibility.

Above all, computer professionals should do the best work they are capable of doing. No matter what the job, employees should do the work they were hired to do. If a person feels that he or she can't perform appropriately, the proper approach is to find another position. Behaving like a professional is the key to succeeding in any field.

algorithm A set of steps for accomplishing a task.

application A computer program that performs a single function, such as a word processing program.

artificial intelligence The branch of computer science concerned with developing computer systems that can learn and make decisions.

biometric identification system An electronic system that uses physical attributes for identification, such as palm prints or scans of the eye.

curriculum A list of courses covered in an academic program.

database A collection of computerized records or data.

data mining Analyzing large volumes of data to find significant trends.

drone An unmanned military vehicle used for scouting.

e-commerce Business that is conducted over the Internet, such as the online sale of products and services.

enterprise resource management The integration of all the computing resources of an organization in order to make information available to the entire company.

facial recognition software A computer program that analyzes the shape of a person's face and compares it to a database of photos for identification.

innovation Coming up with new ideas or advances.

integrated system A combination of devices connected to each other to form a system used for a particular purpose, such as security.

mobile device A computerized device designed to be carried in a purse or pocket that connects to electronic applications wirelessly.

module A stand-alone part of a larger system or program.

multimedia Content that combines different kinds of media, such as visual images and audio.

network A group of interconnected computers.

peripheral A device that attaches to a computer, such as a printer.

photovoltaic panel A device containing solar cells, which convert sunlight into electricity.

prototype A sample version of a product that is produced for testing and evaluation purposes.

robotics The science of automating machines.

server A powerful computer that provides data and services to networked computers.

social networking site A Web site designed to allow people to interact with one another on a personal (as opposed to business) basis.

streaming video Video that is continuously sent over the Internet to a computerized device.

wireless communication Technology that connects electronic applications such as phone services, e-mail, and the Internet by signals sent through the air, rather than over electric wires.

Association of Computer Machinery (ACM)
2 Penn Plaza, Suite 701
New York, NY 10121-0701
(800) 342-6626
Web site: http://www.acm.org
This organization runs special interest groups that work on
specific areas of computer science, maintains a career
center, and offers online books and courses for members.
It accepts student members.

American Society for Engineering Education (ASEE)
1818 N Street NW, Suite 600
Washington, DC 20036-2479
(202) 331-3500
Web site: http://www.asee.org
This organization provides technology education and career
resources for students grades K–12, including a student
newsletter, magazine, blog, and career center.

Computer History Museum
1401 N. Shoreline Boulevard
Mountain View, CA 94043
(650) 810-1010
Web site: http://www.computerhistory.org
In addition to providing exhibits on-site at the museum, this
organization maintains an illustrated history of the computer online.

Computing Technology Industry Association (CompTIA)
1815 S. Meyers Road, Suite 300
Oakbrook Terrace, IL 60181-5228
(630) 678-8300
Web site: http://www.comptia.org
This association of businesses involved in information technology around the world provides information on IT in
a variety of fields, such as health care IT, green IT, and
security, and it maintains an educational foundation.

Entertainment Software Association of Canada
130 Spadina Avenue, Suite 408
Toronto, ON M5V 2L4
Canada
(416) 620-7171
Web site: http://www.theesa.ca
This organization provides reports on such areas as the state
of the computer game industry in Canada, as well as news
related to entertainment software.

Information Technology Association of Canada
5090 Explorer Drive, Suite 801
Mississauga, ON L4W 4T9
Canada
(905) 602-8345
Web site: http://www.itac.ca
This organization sponsors a variety of forums on IT topics,
publishes research reports on various aspects of the IT
industry in Canada, and provides the latest news on its
Web site.

International Electrical and Electronics Engineers–
   Student Branch
1828 L Street NW, Suite 1202
Washington, DC 20036-5104
(800) 678-4333
Web site: http://www.ieee.org/web/membership/students/
   index1.html
This organization provides educational and career resources
   for the use of students in computer and technology fields.

Software and Information Industry Association (SIIA)
1090 Vermont Avenue NW, 6th Floor
Washington DC 20005-4095
(202) 289-7442
Web site: http://www.siia.net
This organization offers a variety of daily and weekly newsletters on the software industry, as well as informational
   meetings and Web casts.

WEB SITES

Due to the changing nature of Internet links, Rosen Publishing
has developed an online list of Web sites related to the subject
of this book. This site is updated regularly. Please use this link
to access the list:

http://www.rosenlinks.com/cict/ccsp

For Further Reading

Bolles, Richard M. *What Color Is Your Parachute?: A Practical Manual for Job-Hunters and Career-Changers.* Berkeley, CA: Ten Speed Press, 2009.

Eberts, Marjorie, and Margaret Gisler. *Careers for Computer Buffs and Other Technological Types.* New York, NY: McGraw-Hill, 2006.

Farr, Michael. *Top 100 Computer and Technical Careers.* 4th ed. Indianapolis, IN: JIST Publishing, 2009.

Ford, Jerry Lee. *Programming for the Absolute Beginner.* Boston, MA: Course Technology, 2007.

Gralla, Preston. *How Personal and Internet Security Works.* New York, NY: Que Publishing/Pearson Technology, 2006.

Gralla, Preston, and Eric Lindley. *How Wireless Works.* New York, NY: Que Publishing/Pearson Technology, 2005.

Grebler, Eric B. *3D Game Programming for Teens.* Boston, MA: Course Technology/Thomson Learning, 2006.

InfoTech Employment. "Information Technology Jobs in America." New York, NY: InfoTech Employment, 2009.

Kirk, Amanda. *Field Guides to Finding a New Career: Information Technology.* New York, NY: Checkmark Books/Facts on File, 2009.

McGraw-Hill. *Resumes for Computer Careers.* New York, NY: McGraw-Hill, 2008.

Miller, Michael. *Absolute Beginner's Guide to Computer Science.* New York, NY: Que Publishing/Pearson Technology, 2009.

Mongan, John, Noah Suojanen, and Eric Giguère. *Programming Interviews Exposed: Secrets to Landing Your Next Job.* 2nd ed. Hoboken, NJ: Wiley Publishing, 2007.

Moreira, Paula. *Ace the IT Interview.* New York, NY: McGraw-Hill, 2007.

Moreira, Paula. *Ace the IT Résumé: Résumés and Cover Letters to Get You Hired.* New York, NY: McGraw-Hill, 2007.

Sethi, Maneesh. *Game Programming for Teens.* Boston, MA: Course Technology/Cengage Learning, 2006.

Strelechy, David. *Ferguson's Careers in Focus: Computers.* New York, NY: Ferguson Publishing Co., 2008.

Wang, Wallace. *Beginning Programming for Dummies.* Hoboken, NJ: Wiley Publishing, 2006.

White, Ron, and Timothy Edward Downs. *How Computers Work.* New York, NY: Que Publishing/Pearson Technology, 2007.

Wolfinger, Anne. *Best Career and Education Web Sites.* 6th ed. Indianapolis, IN: JIST Publishing, 2009.

Bibliography

Anonopoulos, Andreas. "Green Enterprise: Three Networking Investments That Make a Difference." TechTarget, October 10, 2009. Retrieved December 1, 2009 (http://searchnetworking. techtarget.com/tip/0,289483,sid7_gci1371020_ mem1,00.html?track=NL-81&ad=737957&Offer=mn_eh 120109NETWUNSC&asrc=EM_USC_10148182& uid=9401860).

Berry, Charles W., and William H. Hawn Jr. *Computer & Internet Dictionary for Ages 9–99.* Hauppauge, NY: Barron's, 2000.

Burns, Julie Kling. *Opportunities in Computer Careers.* New York, NY: McGraw-Hill, 2002.

Carr, Nicholas G. *Does IT Matter? Information Technology and the Corrosion of Competitive Advantage.* Boston, MA: Harvard Business Press, 2004.

Dubie, Denise. "Security Pros Seek Hacking, Forensics Skills." *Network World*, November 9, 2009. Retrieved November 15, 2009 (http://www.networkworld.com/ news/2009/110909-security-skills.html).

Gilster, Ron. *Cisco Networking for Dummies.* Hoboken, NJ: Wiley Publishing, 2002.

Hillstrom, Kevin. *Defining Moments: The Internet Revolution.* Detroit, MI: Omnigraphics, Inc., 2005.

Kearns, Dave. "Effective Identity Management Begins with Your Employees." *Network World*, December 3, 2008. Retrieved December 9, 2009 (http://www.networkworld. com/newsletters/dir/2008/120108id2.html).

Lancaster, Tom. "Network Engineering Overview: Techniques for Making Changes." TechTarget, August 21, 2006. Retrieved November 16, 2009 (http://searchnetworking. techtarget.com/tip/0,289483,sid7_gci1211274,00.html).

Lewis, Bob. *Keep the Joint Running: A Manifesto for 21st Century Information Technology*. Eden Prairie, MN: Survivor Publishing, 2009.

Lewis, Bob. *Learning IT: The Toughest Job in the World*. Eden Prairie, MN: Survivor Publishing, 2004.

Litchko, James P., and Al Payne. *Know Cyber Risk: By Managing Your IT Security*. Rockville, MD: Know Book Publishing, 2004.

Litchko, James P., Ron Lander, and Lew Wagner. *Cyber Threat Levels Response Handbook*. Rockville, MD: Know Book Publishing, 2004.

McGillicuddy, Shamus. "New Skills Emerge for Network Engineering and Administration Careers." TechTarget, June 18, 2009. Retrieved November 7, 2009 (http://searchnetworking.techtarget.com/news/article/0,289142,sid7_gci1359629,00.html).

Morris, Michael. "More Thoughts on Network Engineers and the CCDE." *Network World*, November 5, 2007. Retrieved January 11, 2010 (http://www.networkworld. com/community/node/21969).

Oltsik, Jon. "Networking Nuggets and Security Snippets." *Network World*, January 8, 2010. Retrieved January 11, 2010 (http://www.networkworld.com/community/node/50819).

Plotnick, Neil. "Testing and Planning for New Products." TechTarget, November 20, 2005. Retrieved November 16, 2009 (http://searchnetworking.techtarget.com/

loginMembersOnly/1,289498,sid7_gci782701,00.
html?NextURL=http%3A//searchnetworking.
techtarget.com/tip/0%2C289483%2Csid7_gci782701_
tax305162%2C00.html&app_code=90&).

Ross, John. *Network Know-How.* San Francisco, CA: No
Scratch Press, 2009.

Scarpati, Jessica. "Network Security Risks Multiply
When Enterprises Begin Outsourcing." TechTarget,
October 7, 2009. Retrieved December 1, 2009.
(http://searchnetworking.techtarget.com/news/
article/0,289142,sid7_gci1370642,00.html).

Viega, John. *The Myths of Security: What the Computer Security
Industry Doesn't Want You to Know.* Sebastopol, CA:
O'Reilly Media, 2009.

Index

ABOUT THE AUTHOR

Jeri Freedman has a B.A. degree from Harvard University. For fifteen years, she worked for high-technology companies involved in cutting-edge technologies. She is the author of more than thirty young adult nonfiction books, including *Digital Career Building Through Skinning and Modding* and *Cyber Citizenship and Cyber Safety: Intellectual Property* for Rosen Publishing.

PHOTO CREDITS

Cover (front and back), p. 1 © www.istockphoto.com/ Andrey Prokhorov; cover (front inset) Stephen Brashear/ Getty Images; p. 7 Image Source/Getty Images; pp. 13, 30 Bloomberg via Getty Images; pp. 14, 37 Justin Sullivan/ Getty Images; pp. 17, 25, 64 Shutterstock.com; p. 21 Jetta Productions/Lifesize/Getty Images; p. 27 Chien-min Chung/Getty Images; p. 35 Paul J. Richards/AFP/Getty Images; pp. 45, 49 AFP/Getty Images; p. 51 Time & Life Pictures/Getty Images; p. 53 Jim Watson/AFP/Getty Images; p. 60 Ralph Morse/Time & Life Pictures/Getty Images.

Designer: Matthew Cauli;
Photo Researcher: Peter Tomlinson